The Grand Canyon

For Brannon, at last!—M. D. B.

To George—J. W.

SIMON SPOTLIGHT
An imprint of Simon & Schuster Children's Publishing Division
1230 Avenue of the Americas, New York, NY 10020
Text copyright © 2006 by Marion Dane Bauer
Illustrations copyright © 2006 by John Wallace
All rights reserved, including the right of reproduction
in whole or in part in any form.
SIMON SPOTLIGHT, READY-TO-READ, and colophon
are registered trademarks of Simon & Schuster, Inc.
Manufactured in China 0916 SDI

The Grand Canyon

By **Marion Dane Bauer**

Illustrated by **John Wallace**

Ready-to-Read

Simon Spotlight

New York London Toronto Sydney New Delhi

Water was one of the forces
that made the Grand Canyon.

Water gathered into a river.

The river carried sand,
gravel, even boulders.

The water and sand
and gravel and boulders
cut through rock.
That is the way
every river is born.

But how did this river
make such a deep canyon?

While the water cut down,
the rock lifted up.
Why?

The crust of our earth
is made of big plates.

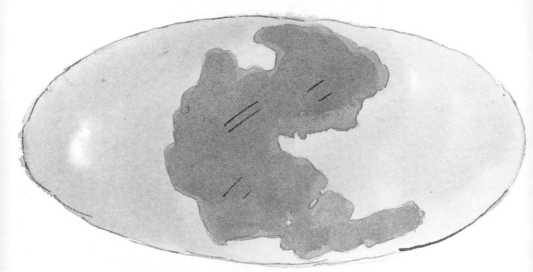

(225 million years ago)

(135 million years ago)

These plates are
always moving.

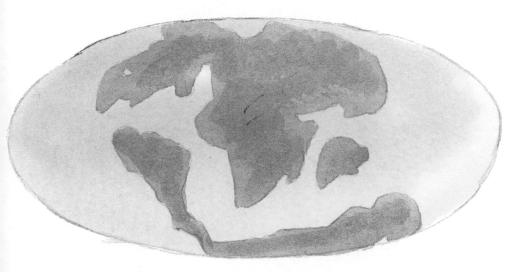

(65 million years ago)

(present)

Where the Grand Canyon
now stands,
one plate pushed
beneath another.

The top plate lifted up
into a high, flat table.

But as the table lifted,
the water kept
cutting through.

That is why we have such a
deep canyon now.
All this happened
in rock time,
very, very slowly.

Theodore Roosevelt
was the first president
to visit the Grand Canyon.

He called it
"one of the great sights
which every American . . .
should see."

It is not only Americans
who want to see the canyon.

North Rim
Visitor Center

Every year five million
people from all over
the world visit
the Grand Canyon.

Some ride mules down
into the canyon.

Some hike down
the steep walls.

Some ride the river
in rafts.

Some stay at the top
and peer down and down
and down.

Everyone admires
this amazing canyon.

Interesting Facts about the Grand Canyon

★ The Grand Canyon is 277 miles long. In some places it is more than a mile deep.

★ The walls of the Grand Canyon are like pages in a book. Each kind of rock makes a page. Scientists can read the book. They can see how each kind of rock was laid down long, long ago.

★ The deepest rock is the oldest. Rocks at the south rim are 250 million years old. Rocks at the bottom are 1.7 billion years old. They lie in colorful layers like a rock rainbow.

★ In 1869, John Wesley Powell was the first white explorer to travel the entire length of the Grand Canyon. He gave the canyon its present name.

★ The canyon has been here for 6 million years. Indians made their homes in it long before white explorers came. Today some of the Havasupai (Ha-va-soo-pi) Indians still live in the canyon.

★ Three types of rocks in the Grand Canyon are limestone, sandstone, and shale. Limestone was formed in a long-ago sea. Sandstone was formed in a desert. Shale was formed from mud.